3-9-99

3-16-99

D0115201

Prayer-Walking

A Simple Path to Body-and-Soul Fitness

Linus Mundy

ABBEY PRESS

© 1994 by St. Meinrad Archabbey
Published by Abbey Press
St. Meinrad, Indiana 47577

Cover and interior design by Scott Wannemuehler

Library of Congress Catalog Number
93-072446

ISBN 0-87029-264-1

Printed in the United States of America

Dedication

To my children, Mike, Emily, and Pat,
who teach me how to walk—and pray.
And to my wife, Mikie,
who lovingly shares the journey.

CONTENTS

Preface...ix
Introduction: Getting Started 3
Step One: Retreat 11
Step Two: Re-Think..........................19
Step Three: Remember—and
    Re-Invent 31
Step Four: Repent 37
Step Five: Return, Repeat.................43
Conclusion 47
Appendix:
    Suggestions for *Your* Prayer-Walk ...51
Bibliography 54

"*Come, you strollers and boulevardiers. You flaneurs, distance demons, and armchair wanderers. Wonderful things are on the horizon.*"

—Ron Strickland,

Shank's Mare: A Compendium of Remarkable Walks

PREFACE

This little book is about "taking a stroll with your soul," a simple, natural method for growing spiritually as you're "going" physically. Prayer-walking is not a new idea, by any means, but it's one that has perhaps been lying out there "under-discovered" long enough.

Prayer-walking is something that most everyone who is blessed with reasonable health can do. Even better, one doesn't have to be terribly coordinated to walk and pray at the same time. (Though it does take some discipline, and we'll get to that later.)

The idea of writing about a prayer-walk came to me one day after I had just completed one. Though I had prayer-walked before, this was the first time I realized that's what I was doing. This time it hit me that I had truly found something holy and Holy out there on the walking trail...something I've gone back for again and again. The experience felt good and right—and frankly, pretty dramatic. Once you begin your prayer-walking, chances are you too will want to return often for the dramatic benefits.

Speaking of benefits, why did I begin prayer-walking? Truthfully, I think I can say, "My culture made me do it!" Here in the Western world, we love to be as efficient, effective, and practical as we can be. And if there's a chance to do two things at once, we'll take it. If we can make money at a job and have it be satisfying and fulfilling too, we'll take it. If we can play with our children at the same time we turn the pages of the newspaper, we'll do it. If we can drop the kids off at soccer practice and drive through the park to enjoy it on the way home, we'll do that. (Well, maybe, if it's not too far out of the way. Chances are, we'll drive through the "drive-through" instead. That's more practical!)

The trouble is that accomplishing the practical is what we are really good at; the spiritual (which seems like the "impractical") then becomes secondary. Rarely do we think about putting the practical and the spiritual together. I know I exercised for years motivated primarily by the physical benefits: how I'd feel better, be thinner, be stronger, maybe even live longer. Once in a while when I was exercising, I'd become aware of the spiritual side of my actions, the "centering down" as the Quakers call it. I'd have spiritual thoughts. But they were pretty "accidental" and spontaneous, certainly not intentional. As with most folks, work and play, the physical and the spiritual, had separate places in my life.

Prayer-walking brings body-and-soul benefits together, at the same time and in a truly efficient way. It doesn't put prayer in one place and walking (that is, exercising) in another. Ahhh. Efficiency. We like that. Of course, efficiency isn't the reason to pray. But if efficiency is a motivation that works for you—as it was for me—I'm glad to suggest it as one. Looking for better motivations? I hope you'll find them on the following pages. Thanks for coming along.

"*When I was a little girl...my mother took us kids for prayer walks out in the country—in the summertime, after supper. I've been walking into the world ever since. And while my walks with my mother were in silence, there was a whole lot of talking going on. The world was telling me about itself, about myself, and about the mystery permeating everything.*"

—Jose Hobday, *Praying magazine*

INTRODUCTION

———✦———

Getting Started

I recently saw an advertisement for a nifty, comfortable-looking pair of shoes in *Walking* magazine. The type read: "Walking isn't just good for your heart. It's good for your soul." That's the premise of this book.

This past year I've had this premise powerfully reconfirmed. A man whom I have long revered, T George Harris, came into the lives of our publishing team here at Abbey Press. (Thank you, friend,

William "Ace" Remas, for a kind and for-
tuitous introduction.) Harris, as many
readers may know, was the editor of
Psychology Today magazine, which did
much the same thing we're trying to do in
this small volume: bring the ordinary and
the extraordinary, the sacred and the secu-
lar, closer together. What Harris and his
team did for psychology in the '70s and
'80s, we at Abbey Press aspire to help do
for religion and spirituality in the '90s and
beyond: make them more and more accessible to "non-specialists." (That's people
like me.)

T George's remarkable work today more
than ever promotes this alliance and inter-
relationship of mind-body-spirit. Thus I
am especially grateful for his editorial con-
tribution to this *Prayer-Walking* volume.
His wisdom and experience are especially

evidenced in this book's preface and in chapter two. It is in the latter where Harris so beautifully assists in explaining the wonderful blending of the scientific and the sacred that's been going on. Indeed, it was Harris himself whose efforts prompted an $800,000 research project to substantiate the thesis stated a few paragraphs above: "Walking isn't just good for your heart. It's good for your soul."

So, having said all this, what makes prayer-walking so healthful for body and soul? Is it that prayer-walking helps us get away from it all...so that we can find it all?

Writer Joseph Gallagher says we often don't hear our own selves above the clang and clatter of our daily lives. "We keep our lives so noisy," says he, "that we can't eavesdrop on the secret murmurings of our own hearts."

What's unfortunate is that these secret murmurings are invariably about eternal things, things which matter the most. The murmurings are about life and death, God and goodness, suffering and salvation, love and wonder.

Conversely, what drowns out these truly important concerns are usually, as we know, life's loud and less lofty matters. They are the things which steal our attention—like making money or preparing a meal or getting ourselves or our children to and fro.

This is not to say that some of the clang and clatter drowning out the eternal matters is unimportant. "What's for lunch?" "When's the deadline?" "What do you want, son?" are all important questions, even if they're not eternal ones.

But the point is: The clang and clatter

will continue to dominate our lives unless we do something different. We need to make a choice that can deliver us from our routines—and our routine selves.

Many good options are available, some much more doable than others. (An intensive, six-week retreat every other six weeks, for example, or reading the entire *Summa Theologica* of Thomas Aquinas during summer vacation can certainly deliver us from our routines, but the side effects of such spiritual discipline could be rather devastating!) The choice I am advocating is a more practical one, I think. It's called "taking a trip"—not far from where you are. Periodically, regularly, systematically, we can "walk away" from our noisy trappings and disturbing distractions, if we have the will and discipline to do so.

By walking away, we walk *toward* something invaluable—what we might call a new way of being, a new reality, a new appreciation of something eternal.

———•◆•———

There is a saying that a journey of a thousand miles begins with one step. One of the first steps on this "thousand-mile journey" is to put on your walking shoes (any comfortable pair will do). But before you start walking, I suggest you consider each of the five recommendations that follow in the next very short chapters of this book. They can help bring you to the greater holiness and wholeness that you're seeking.

———•◆•———

What will actually happen on your prayer-walks? Often you will hear the message in the murmurings buried inside your heart. And once in a while, you will realize those murmurings are coming not only from *your* heart—but from *God's* heart.

"

. . . [What] within walls seems improbable or incredible, outdoors seems merely natural. That is because outdoors we are confronted everywhere with wonders; we see that the miraculous is not extraordinary, but the common mode of existence. It is our daily bread."

—Wendell Berry, poet, essayist, farmer

CHAPTER ONE

Step One: Retreat

"I am closer to God in a field or woods or garden than anywhere else," to paraphrase a great many poets and naturalists who find the Divine by stepping back and stepping out. Trappist monk and writer Thomas Merton, who lived in a silent hermitage for most of the three years before his death, observed: "No writing on the solitary, meditative dimension of life can say anything that has not already been said better by the wind in the pine trees."

I myself have been privileged to hear the wind in the same pine trees where Thomas Merton listened. The Abbey of Gethsemani, set among the hills and forests of Kentucky, is a favorite place of retreat for me. But the truth is: The wind also speaks in the trees where *you* are. Go, retreat to those trees, or to the hills, the beach, the park, the farm, the cemetery, the neighborhood, or the garden, and walk there with your God in prayer. Nature will bring you the nurture you seek. God will be available there—and you will be available to God.

What do you do if nature is not readily available to you? If your backyard is too small or uninteresting? If your uncle's farm is three states away and the park not exactly next door either? Nature is where you find it and, like beauty, is in the eye of the beholder. The school or church grounds or the shopping center near your home or workplace may be less than totally "natural," but they *are* accessible. (And there's always the possibility of *human* nature inspiring you at those locations!)

In my own experience and that of many walkers I know, it's usually not *place* that's the biggest problem; it's lack of *resolve*. And, ironically, where is one of the best places to find resolve? In nature!

When I was a student of American literature in college, a literary movement called "literary naturalism" almost did me in (literally). So much of the great writing of that movement preached realism and fatalism. This was depressing stuff, indeed, and yet it had a real ring of truth to the scientific, fact-seeking side of me. But especially intriguing to me was what I found so many of these writers "had instead of God" (in Ernest Hemingway's phrase)—*nature.* It was only nature that they could count on, fall back on, retreat to, in their worst of times.

As people of faith, we can have God *and* nature—and God *in* nature—to rely on. We believe with the psalmist that "the heavens declare the glory of God, and the firmament proclaims God's handiwork" (Psalm 19:1). And even though God is beyond anything we can see, touch, taste, or smell—even in nature—we can encounter many a glimpse of God's available grandeur in the "wild."

Oddly enough, it is there—amid the outdoor feast for our senses—that we can better, as Merton puts it, "answer the secret voice of God calling us to take a risk and venture by faith *outside the reassuring and protective limits of our five senses*" (my emphasis).

It is when we get outside our senses that we approach the Divine. That sounds a bit like risky business to most of us who are inclined (reclined?) to accept and welcome the safety of the couch, evening TV, the daily newspaper, a best-selling novel.

Why "risky"? Because we may come to some disturbing conclusions about our lives or ourselves; we may realize just how effortful spiritual growth can be—and we may not want to have to work that hard. M. Scott Peck in *The Road Less Traveled* emphasizes that once we discover the "God within us," we usually find ourselves being urged to take the more difficult path, "the path of more effort rather than less." That is the "warning" all of us prayer-walkers must deal with: the "farther" or "deeper" we go on our walks, the "farther" or "deeper" we may be challenged (and feel obligated) to go within ourselves.

Don't get me wrong. God's grandeur (and the "wild") are certainly present at home, too. But for many of us it is only in retreating from our daily worlds for a while, as Jesus did when he "went out into the hills to pray," that we can see that all of life is holy and blessed, including the noise and the disorder and the ordinariness "back home." We leave this ordinariness only to come back and see everything with new eyes.

Writer Edward Hays reports that since the mid-1960s an entire library of books has been written about various methods for prayer and meditation. "While the methods and practices are many, they are all directed towards the same end, namely, to still the flow of thoughts and desires that keep the mind and heart constantly occupied and thus to make one more available to God." Getting out on a prayer-walk is sure to make your mind and heart more "available."

———

The phrase "communing with nature" is a good one. When you make yourself available to nature, nature makes itself available to you. And God is there for the asking.

"The world is charged with the grandeur of God.
It will flame out, like shining from shook foil;
It gathers to a greatness, like the ooze of oil Crushed....
And for all this, nature is never spent;
There lives the dearest freshness deep down things;..."

—Gerard Manley Hopkins,
"God's Grandeur"

CHAPTER TWO

Step Two: Re-Think

We have jammed busy-busy doings into all the nooks and crannies of life. You have to be seventy to remember farm life before tractors and electrical power took over enough of the muscle work to let us work much longer hours, mainly with our minds. As long as the body had to rest from, say, wrestling with a turning plow from sun to sun, most men and women were forced to rest their minds along with their exhausted bodies. When you hoed corn all week, Sunday was indeed a blessed day to rest the body/mind.

The world we now live in operates more by the clock than by the sun and seasons. It leaves few spaces between things we do, and those spaces left are quickly filled up with TV, newspapers, commercials, our own sense of trying harder to be at our best. We try hard to make even our play "productive."

And we push each other. Even before our children go to first grade, we start prepping them to make it into the tougher universities. The old-fashioned idea of a long, leisurely vacation is fading before a rising habit of short, fast trips which are supposed to somehow jump-start our energies and get us back into peak performance.

The pressures are rising, many of them

computer-driven. In the hot, young high-tech companies of California, CEOs with Ph.D.'s in many fields play a savage game of basketball at noon so as to "be up at peak intensity for head work all afternoon," as one of them explains. The physical exercise sure helps, since stress at its worst is mental tension with no physical outlet, no release in fight or flight.

But the mind needs a break as much as the body does. Because mental stress became so deadly, it was a medical scientist, Harvard cardiologist Herbert Benson, who began in the '60s to study how to cope with it all. Every major culture, he found, had some kind of repetitive song or ritual or prayer that creates what he calls "the Relaxation Response," the opposite of the fight or flight response.

Just repeating a word over and over, he

proved in experiments, keeps the mind occupied so that it doesn't keep racing around a single set of worries. The body returns to a kind of stasis, to normal operating health. Heart rate goes down, as does blood pressure if it has been too high, along with adrenaline and metabolism and a batch of related alarms. As Benson began testing out the medical benefits of these "stress buster" techniques, he realized just why they had been built into our spiritual tradition long before today's more urgent need for them.

These "stress busters" are shade trees for the spirit. In years of research, Dr. Benson has now found significant reductions in many diseases and most pains among patients who evoke the Relaxation Response, even if they do so by repeating a neutral word like "one" over and over or by counting every breath they take.

The trouble is, however, that such a neutral process can bore you to death. Even terminal cancer patients would drop out of meditation programs when required to repeat a pointless word ad nauseam. Benson admitted his mistake and helped his patients come up with a word, phrase, or sentence that meant something, if possible something very important and spiritual.

In effect, he was asking them to come up with a prayer.

He pointedly did not omit atheists. Some chose "Peace be with you," or just "Peace." Jews often used "Shalom," Protestants their favorite lines, many and varied. Many Catholics would repeat "Hail Mary, full of grace..."

Meanwhile, out at Long Beach State in California, Robert Thayer was finding what we've all known in our bones but never expected medicine to understand: Taking a walk actually makes you feel better.

As a psychologist, Dr. Thayer found that we also get a mood boost from eating a candy bar, but the sugar soon lets us down so we feel worse than before. Many stimulants, like caffeine, also drop us later. But a walk takes us up without making us drop later. Thayer began to recommend that his students take a ten-minute walk before intense study, before a test, whenever.

The two lines of discovery, Benson's and Thayer's, needed to be combined, and a dedicated family in Minneapolis generously funded a major research project in the Boston area. (Author's note: It was thanks especially to the efforts of T George Harris that this project got off the ground.) Two years and $800,000 later, Dr. Benson had clear evidence that a prayer-walk not only boosts your mood but also gives your mind that rest from stress—the Relaxation Response—with its host of body benefits. Both mind and body benefit from healthy spirituality.

While generations of theologians, spiritual writers, and practitioners have done deep analysis of prayer and its religious function, nobody had ever before done rigorous physiological and psychological studies such as these.

We are creatures of our age. Few of us can find the restful moments we so urgently need. We can, however, do walking prayers, or prayer-walks, to hold off the barrage of stress that hits us from all sides but mainly rises inside ourselves.

When the wisdom of the spirit combines with the hard evidence of medicine, we have a fairly clear invitation to go out and enjoy ourselves on foot. Whether you drive yourself into a race-walk or stroll in the woods for mindful meditation, an old pair of shoes can take you into a healthy new feeling and state.

———=◆=———

The Lord wants us to "have life and have it more abundantly." There's hardly a better way to prove that there's life in our bodies than by moving them. (Sometimes the proof continues the day after, when we feel our muscles in pain.) The point is that moving the body, walking, exercising have been proven to be healthy and life-giving, even life-extending.

"Voluntary walking is not a rejection of

technology [the automobile, bus, etc.] as much as it is a reaffirmation of the pleasure of having two legs," says Ron Strickland in his introduction to *Shank's Mare*, a wonderful and unusual book which collects the adventures of famous and not-so-famous "walkers," ranging from naturalist and writer Edward Abbey to Winston Churchill, Neil Armstrong, and Anaïs Nin. They speak of the exhilaration, the euphoria, the *spirituality* (my translation—and sometimes theirs) which walking can offer. "A century ago," says Strickland, "someone feeling this way would 'light out for the territory' or stampede off on the latest gold rush." Today they "light out" for the hiking trails, the woods or pasture, the city or suburban sidewalks. Many of them are prayer-walking—and some of them know it.

Because of new research this year at Stanford University, even aerobics-loving Jane Fonda now urges short, happy walks rather than long, harsh workouts. The good things which happen chemically—the release of endorphins, for example, which provide a sense of well-being; the muscle tone, which can ward off injuries; the increased lung capacity and function, which improve both our stamina and our comfort—are complemented with good things happening spiritually. Prayer-walking fills the bill as that ideal exercise for body and soul.

Good walking and good praying can go together. Taking a prayer-walk can become a part—an enjoyable part—of your total spiritual fitness program. "All real prayer leads us to increasing self-awareness," writes A.W. Richard Sipe in the periodical

Fellowship in Prayer. A prayer-walk is something in which you can involve your mind, your body, your spirit—together. Growth in self-awareness—steady, rewarding growth—is the natural by-product.

There's an additional benefit. When you're walking, your forward motion sort of brings the future toward you and pushes the past behind. When you're *prayer*-walking, however, the sense of *now* is the dominant one, not the future or the past. And you're making the now *holy*.

"*I have met but one or two persons in the course of my life who understood the art of walking...who had a genius, so to speak, for sauntering.*"

—Henry David Thoreau

CHAPTER THREE

Step Three: Remember— and Re-Invent

When I was a child, we used to take formal prayer-walks. Back then we called them "processions" or "pilgrimages." On given Sundays, we would parade on foot through the "aisles" of a huge apple orchard. These were church-sponsored affairs, and we walked as a family, praying the Rosary, with hundreds of fellow Christians, honoring Mary, the Mother of Jesus. They were simple devotions, and there was a simple holiness about them.

31

In parochial school, and even in the high school I attended, we would have prayerful processions (or, at least, the intentions were prayerful!). These "group" prayer-walks brought yet another experience of communing...not only uniting with nature and aspiring to unite with the Divine, but also uniting with one another as we proceeded (processed) with a common purpose on a common route toward a common destination.

Some pilgrimages and processions continue to be held to this day, but they are few and far between. One dramatic "group prayer-walk" comes to mind. In Mexico City on the feast of Our Lady of Guadalupe, pilgrims and natives alike proceed on their knees to a full-house worship service as a demonstration of spiritual devotion. Though I myself have not been present to this, a dear friend of mine has felt the great power and sense of community that arises on this prayer-walk.

Political marches for peace and justice issues can also be beautiful examples of "group prayer-walks"—advocating Gospel values in a very visible and expressive manner.

T George Harris was present at that most famous 1960s "March on Washington." He recalls the gentle reverence that pervaded the thousands of walkers before Martin Luther King's moving "I have a dream" oration.

Locating and joining a procession—or even organizing such a pilgrimage or walk or march with your friends, neighbors, church community—can be a powerful experience—and perhaps not as difficult to arrange or participate in as you might at first think. Something as simple as a neighbors-and-friends Christmas caroling night can turn out to be a wonderfully prayerful group experience.

———✧———

However scarce the opportunities for such community prayer-walks, there is one pilgrimage you can always count on. And that is the personal pilgrimage you yourself "re-invent" on a quiet, solo prayer-walk.

One more thing about remembering. The beauty is that as you persevere in your prayer-walks, you will build up memories of how the landscape—and you—change over time. As the weeks, months, and years pass, you will look back realizing you have re-invented a simple spiritual path toward holiness not unlike what you may have experienced as a child.

"*We must somehow take a wider view, look at the whole landscape, really see it, and describe what's going on here. Then we can at least wail the right question into the swaddling band of darkness or, if it comes to that, choir the proper praise.*"
—Annie Dillard, *Pilgrim at Tinker Creek*

CHAPTER FOUR

◆━◆━◆

Step Four: Repent

Much of what we have written thus far on the value of prayer-walking is about our feeling closer to God. But evangelist Billy Graham, for one, says God doesn't just want us to feel closer—to take "just a closer walk with thee." Rather, God wants us to learn what holy plan God has for each of us. We do this, says Rev. Graham, by receiving God's Word—and repenting.

This repentance—which I like to call

conversion, that change of mind and heart which we spoke of earlier in chapter one— is much of what we can do on a prayer-walk. When we go out on the trail, wherever it may be (but especially if it is in a wooded or otherwise natural setting), we drastically change our environment from the usual surroundings we know. We can readily see that "we're not in Kansas anymore," that this is not, for instance, our home or office, with all its trappings and routines. Out there we see how *change* can be *good*. We can appreciate the physical change—that one's easy. But we can also open up more, we can become more receptive, to the much more difficult change of heart and mind which Scripture calls us to.

What are these necessary changes? You will find yours on your prayer-walk, as I am finding mine. In the appendix, I describe what to take along on your prayer-walk. One recommendation that comes to mind in this context: Have a pertinent Scripture passage, one that speaks to the type of conversion you may have identified as necessary for yourself.

Reflecting on something as simple, and profound, as God's two great commandments—love God, love your neighbor as yourself—will take me a long, long way down the trail.

Another appropriate text might be the Lord's Prayer, or "Not my will but thine," an excellent "faith-first" prayer for one and all.

Another good "conversion passage" I value at this time of my life comes from the beginning of the letter of James. The words are about praying with confidence: "But your prayer must be made with faith, and no trace of doubt, because a person who has doubts is like the waves thrown up in the sea by the buffeting of the wind. That sort of person, of two minds, inconsistent in every activity, must not expect to receive anything from the Lord." Prayer-walking helps take me out of that "two minds" mentality. I believe it can do the same for you.

What we need, as the words in an old English hymn suggest, is to walk "more by faith, less by sight." In walking "by faith" and seeking inner conversion, we come to find what really matters in life, what the soul really is seeking. And that is love. Or, more accurately, it is divine love—a relationship with the Divine Lover. That's what we truly hunger for and wish to walk toward.

But where do we find it? How do we

find it? We find it not at the end of the walk but *on the way*. And not just on a *prayer-walk*, but on all our "walks." We learn to recognize it where it already exists: in me and you, in the fat lady and the skinny man, in the big ocean and the little fish, in Mother Earth and in Father Time. It is here—now—in us—on the way. We are on a journey, yes, and there is a destination. But our God who cares for us is not *just* there at the end of our walks. God is near now and with us every step of the way.

"*There are risks on this prayer-walk: Snakes, maybe. Bees. The bull beyond the electric fence. The trees swaying with such force you fear for your life. But then there's the safe side. And lunch at the end of it.*"
—The author's "Gethsemani journal"

CHAPTER FIVE

———◆◆◆———

Step Five: Return, Repeat

The sad part of any good thing, it seems, is that it comes to an end. So when our prayer-walk ends, our prayer ends? Wrong, of course. Physical fitness experts assure us that the effects of any exercise—the metabolic changes—continue long after the exercise itself has stopped.

Incidentally, one of the special benefits of walking is for people who now do almost no exercise. The less you do, the more you benefit from anything you add.

After our repeated prayer-walks, after our repeated "opening-ups" to the spirit, we begin to truly integrate the values we have found and keep finding "out there" and carry them with us wherever we go.

As the self-help experts on practically any subject tell us: Make the commitment; make it a habit; get someone to keep you honest. Obviously, all these tips hold true for prayer-walking. Something becomes a habit when you do it just three times, says one expert. (With our children, just one time makes it a habit—if it was fun!)

The importance of a schedule can't be overemphasized. As spiritual writer David Knight stresses: "You can't just say you're going to become a more prayerful person. You can't even just say you're going to pray more. You have to say you're going to pray on Tuesdays and Thursdays from 7 to

7:15. *Now* you're becoming a more prayerful person. *Now* you're praying more" (my emphasis).

The same holds true for prayer-walking. Schedule your prayer-walks; stick with the schedule. And you'll be praying more—and better.

Once you get into walking, you will gradually move on, from everyday consciousness of everything going on around you into a whole new realm: that blessed space where time stops and you are free of desire and plans, entirely in the *now*. And that's a peaceful place where I truly believe God wants us to live at least some of the time!

"*What our prayer-walk can teach us, really, is that it's all holy ground we walk on—whether that ground is in the laundry room, in the boardroom, or under the roomy skies.*"

— "Taking a Prayer-Walk,"
an Abbey Press *PrayerNote*

CONCLUSION

———◆◆◆———

What do prayer and walking have in common? For many, many years, our society as a whole seems to have viewed both as pretty much a waste of time. They both appeared to accomplish so little. And they didn't work fast enough—if at all.

But the popular wisdom has been changing. Walking—even slow walking—is good for us. "Wasting some time" with God—even a lot of time—is good for us.

Deciding to take a prayer-walk means scheduling a time and a place where God can touch us and we can touch God.

A prayer-walk? Go for it!

"*Take a walk—but don't go anywhere. If you walk just to get somewhere, you sacrifice the walking.*"

—Slow-down Therapy

APPENDIX

———◆◆◆———

Some suggestions for your prayer-walk:

✦ Realize, as you walk, that your real journey is an interior one. You are looking for love and opening up to Grace.

✦ Make it clear to God, and yourself, as you set out that this is a walk *toward* holiness. You are seeking it; you have prayerful *intentions*. Not

finding prayer or holiness with
every step—or every prayer-walk,
for that matter—is not failure. By
your very setting out on a quest,
you please the One you seek.

↞ Make this *your* prayer-walk. That
means walking at your pace, on or
off the marked paths, reciting
traditional prayers, spontaneous
prayer, "centering" prayer, or,
obviously sometimes, "no" prayer.
(You'll always come back home with
something holy, whether you
recognize it at the time or not.)

↞ Things to take along (all optional):
a walking stick, a notebook,
spiritual reading, a pet, a friend, a
child, inspiring music; perhaps most

often, none of the above.

↤ Things to take along (*not* optional):
the cry—or song—in your heart,
the people you love (living and
dead), your dreams, your true self.

↤ Things to take along and "drop
off," bit by bit, on your prayer-
walks: your hurts, your worries,
your false self.

May you and I travel lighter with each
new step!

ADDITIONAL READING

Books

The Relaxation Response, by Dr. Herbert Benson and Miriam Z. Klipper, New York, Avon, 1976.

Shank's Mare: A Compendium of Remarkable Walks, edited by Ron Strickland, New York, Paragon House, 1988.

Pilgrim at Tinker Creek, by Annie Dillard, New York, Harper and Row, 1974.

New Seeds of Contemplation, by Thomas Merton, New York, New Directions, 1961.

Prayers for a Planetary Pilgrim, by Edward Hays, Leavenworth, Kansas, Forest of Peace Books, 1989.

Walking: A Complete Guide to the Complete Exercise, by Casey Meyers, New York, Random House, 1992.

Prayer Therapy, by Keith McClellan, O.S.B., St. Meinrad, Indiana, Abbey Press, 1990.

Joys of the Road: A Little Anthology in Praise of Walking, by Waldo Ralph Browne, Freeport, New York, Books for Libraries Press, 1970.

Magazines
Praying, NCR Publishing Company, Kansas City, Missouri.

Living Prayer, Barre, Vermont.

Fellowship in Prayer, Princeton, New Jersey.

Booklets
PrayerNotes, Abbey Press, St. Meinrad, Indiana.